NATURAL WORLD

KILLER
WHALE

HABITATS • LIFE CYCLES • FOOD CHAINS • THREATS

Mark Carwardine

RSVP

RAINTREE
STECK-VAUGHN
PUBLISHERS
A Steck-Vaughn Company

Austin, Texas

NATURAL WORLD

Chimpanzee • Elephant • Giant Panda • Great White Shark
Killer Whale • Lion • Polar Bear • Tiger

Cover: A killer whale comes up for air.
Title page: An adult killer whale in Antarctica
Contents page: A killer whale breaching
Index page: Two killer whales at the surface

Published by Raintree Steck-Vaughn Publishers,
an imprint of Steck-Vaughn Company

Library of Congress Cataloging-in-Publication Data
Carwardine, Mark.
Killer Whale / Mark Carwardine.
    p.   cm.—(Natural world)
    Includes bibliographical references and index.
    Summary: Introduces the behavior of killer whales
from birth to old age, describing their feeding and
mating habits, social structure, threats, and more.
    ISBN 0-7398-1058-8 (hard)
    0-7398-0949-0 (soft)
    1. Killer whale—Juvenile literature.
    [1. Killer whale. 2. Whales.]
    I. Title. II. Series.
    QL737.C432C335 2000
    599.53'6—dc21   99-18099

Printed in Italy. Bound in the United States.
1 2 3 4 5 6 7 8 9 0 04 03 02 01 00

Picture acknowledgments
Bruce Coleman Collection *front cover*, 1, 8 (Jeff Foott Produc-
tions), 9 (Johnny Johnson), 11 (Jeff Foott Productions), 13 (Pacific
Stock), 15 (Pacific Stock), 16 (Jeff Foott Productions), 18, 20 (Jeff
Foott Productions), 23 (Johnny Johnson), 24 (Jeff Foott Produc-
tions), 29 (Jeff Foott Productions), 30 (Jeff Foott Productions), 32
(Harald Lange), 34 (Johnny Johnson), 36 (Pacific Stock), 37 (Ken
Balcomb), 40 (Mark Carwardine), 44t (Jeff Foott Productions),
45t (Ken Balcomb), 45m (Johnny Johnson), 48; Mark Carwar-
dine *back cover*, 21, 26, 39, 42; Digital Vision 6, 10; Oxford Scien-
tific Films 17 (David B. Fleetham); Still Pictures 7 (Michel Denis-
Huot), 12 (Michel Denis-Huot), 14 (J. P. Sylvestre), 18–19 (Ray
Pfortner), 22–23 (Michel Denis-Huot), 27 (Christophe Guinet),
28 (Mark Carwardine), 33 (Norbert Wu), 35 (Yves Gouedard), 38
(Mark Edwards), 41 (Roland Seitre), 43 (Marilyn Kazmers), 44m
(J.P. Sylvestre), 44b (Mark Carwardine), 45b (Michel Denis-
Huot); Stockmarket 3 (Thomas H. Brakefield). Artwork by
Michael Posen.

Contents

The Killer Whale

The killer whale is a very striking animal and is easy to recognize. Although it is a powerful predator, it should not really be called "killer" at all. Like other hunting animals, such as lions, tigers, and polar bears, the killer whale kills to eat. But unlike these animals, killer whales in the wild do not attack humans. Many experts prefer to call the killer whale by its other name, the "orca."

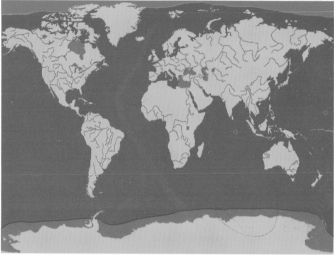

▲ The blue-shaded areas show where killer whales live. They are most common in the freezing cold waters of the polar regions.

KILLER WHALE FACTS

The killer whale's scientific name is *Orcinus orca.*

•

Each killer whale family has its own special language, or dialect.

•

The killer whale is a natural acrobat and often leaps right out of the water.

► An adult killer whale

Dorsal fin

The male killer whale has a huge dorsal fin, which can be up to 6 ft. (1.8 m) tall. The female's dorsal fin is much smaller and more curved.

Blowhole

The killer whale breathes through its blowhole, which is on the top of its head.

Teeth

A killer whale has up to 100 teeth in its mouth. They are all pointed and sharp for seizing and tearing prey.

Saddle-patch

All killer whales have a distinctive gray marking on the back, which varies in shape and brightness from one killer whale to the next.

Pectoral fin

Pectoral fins, or flippers, are used for steering and turning in the water. The killer whale's pectoral fins are shaped like paddles.

Tail

The killer whale is a fast swimmer. It uses its powerful tail to reach speeds of up to 30 mph (50 km/h).

The killer whale belongs to a group of animals known as the cetaceans (pronounced "set-ay-shuns"). All the world's whales, dolphins, and porpoises are cetaceans. Despite its name, the killer whale is actually the largest member of the dolphin family, so perhaps it should have been called the "killer dolphin!"

▼ A common dolphin. The killer whale is a member of the dolphin family. The common dolphin is one of its close relatives.

▲ A family pod of killer whales surfaces to breathe.

Although it is shaped rather like a fish and lives in the sea, the killer whale is a mammal. It cannot breathe underwater and, like us, has lungs instead of gills. Therefore, it has to hold its breath every time it dives and must return to the surface for air.

Birth

It has been about 15 to 17 months since the female killer whale mated. She is now ready to give birth to a baby killer whale, or calf. Her calf is born underwater, near the surface. As soon as it is born, the calf swims up to the surface. Somehow, it knows not to breathe until its blowhole is safely clear of the water.

Killer whales normally have just one calf at a time. When it is first born, the calf looks similar to its mother, but it is not exactly the same. Its saddle-patch is normally darker than its mother's, and its white areas can be reddish in color. But, by the time it is a year old, the calf's coloring will be like that of adult killer whales.

▲ A newborn killer whale calf is enormous —about a third the length of its mother.

▶ A mother and calf swimming side by side

CALVES

A newborn killer whale calf measures about 6.5 ft (2m) long and can weigh as much as 400 lbs.(180 kg)—much bigger than a fully grown human.

●

Calves can swim as soon as they are born, although their movements are a little awkward at first.

Exploring a New World

Under its mother's watchful eye, the calf begins to explore its new underwater home. It soon meets other animals, including a variety of squid, fish, seabirds, seals, and other whales and dolphins. Some of them may be very frightened by the calf and its family, but others may allow it to take a closer look.

▼ The killer whale calf takes great interest in turtles and all the other animals it meets in the sea.

▲ The young calf rarely leaves its mother's side.

Although their mothers take care of them, many killer whale calves die when they are very young. They may die of illness or in accidents, or they may be killed by predators such as large sharks.

11

The Family Group

The killer whale calf will never leave home. Even a fully grown adult male will spend its entire life in a special family group, called a pod. The pod may include the calf's mother, grandmother, half sisters and half brothers, aunts, uncles, and cousins. All the family members feed together, rest together, and travel together.

Only the fathers and grandfathers are missing from the pod. They are living with their mothers in other family groups.

▲ A pod of killer whales resting at the surface

On the average, a pod contains about ten to twelve whales, but there may be as many as fifty. Each pod has its own home range—a favorite area in which its members spend most of their time. This may extend well over a hundred square miles.

The home ranges of different pods often overlap, so the whales often meet. Sometimes they take no notice of each other. But occasionally they join briefly to form a big "superpod." A superpod may contain 150 or more whales.

▼ Killer whales are always on the move and have enormous home ranges.

13

Growing Up

During its first year, a killer whale calf feeds only on its mother's milk. It forms a special feeding tube by holding its tongue against the roof of its mouth. The mother squirts her milk into the tube. The calf is suckled underwater, but near the surface so that both mother and baby can come up for air. Killer whale milk is extremely rich, and it helps the calf grow quickly.

▼ The young calf grows rapidly in its first year.

Killer whales often "spyhop"—they poke their heads out of the water to take a look around.

At about one year old, the calf will begin to eat solid food. Some killer whale pods feed mainly on fish. Others eat almost anything from penguins to other whales. The calf will eat the same food as the other members of its pod. Gradually, over several years, it will stop drinking its mother's milk altogether.

Male and female calves grow at about the same rate until they are nine to ten years old. Then the males grow more than the females. Males can grow to nearly 32 ft. (10 m) long and can weigh up to 10 tons. The females reach a length of up to 28 ft. (8.5 m) and a weight of 6 to 7 tons.

▲ The calf feels safe and secure when it is swimming by its mother's side.

Staying Safe

The killer whale calf sometimes appears to be attached to its mother's side by an invisible thread. The two animals swim side by side, always touching each other. This makes it much more difficult for large sharks to see the calf when they are on the lookout for food.

Young killer whales are too small and inexperienced to look after themselves, especially during a shark attack. They need the protection of their mothers and of other members of the pod.

Adult killer whales have no real predators, and there is nothing in the sea for them to fear. Even great white sharks are not a serious threat. In fact, a killer whale was recently filmed attacking and killing a big great white shark off the coast of California.

▼ Great white sharks may be a danger to very young killer whales, but they are no threat to the adults.

Acrobatics

▼ Killer whales often breach, which means they leap into the air and land back in the water with a tremendous splash.

As it grows, the calf learns and practices many of the skills essential for being an adult killer whale. It learns how to find its way around in the sea, how to communicate with other members of the pod, and how to catch food.

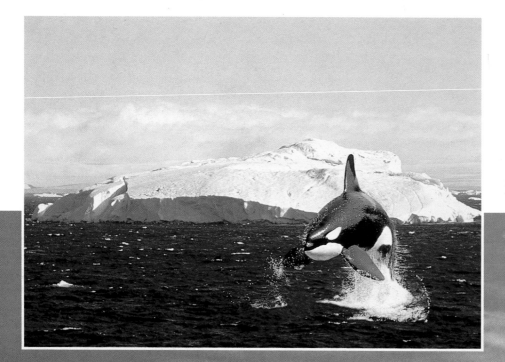

▼ A breaching killer whale off the coast of the state of Washington

The calf must also learn how to behave like a killer whale. Adult killer whales are very active animals and spend a lot of their time doing acrobatics at the surface. They leap high into the air and land back in the water with a tremendous splash. This is called breaching. They also slap the surface with their flippers, fins, and tails, poke their heads out of the water, and play in the waves produced by boats.

BREACHING

No one knows why killer whales breach. They may be herding fish or trying to impress a mate. They may be sending signals to each other, warning other killer whales to stay away, or pointing out a possible source of danger, or they may simply be having fun.

•

Sometimes a killer whale breaches several times in a row. When that happens, other whales may breach as well.

Swimming and Diving

It is several months before a calf can swim as well as the adults. Adult killer whales are fast, efficient swimmers. They can reach speeds of more than 30 mph (50 km/h) and can swim for long periods without a rest. Their powerful tails propel them forward, and their smooth, streamlined bodies help them move easily through the water.

▲ Killer whales can swim faster than any other whales or dolphins.

At first, the calf cannot stay underwater for long. It has to learn how to hold its breath for many minutes at a time. Some adult killer whales can stay underwater for 15 minutes or more.

After a dive, the calf rises to the surface and blows out stale air from its lungs. Sometimes it is possible to see its breath, like a small cloud above the young whale's head. Then it breathes in fresh air before it dives again.

▼ A male killer whale breathes out through the blowhole on the top of its head.

Communicating

Killer whale calves have to learn how to
communicate with other members of the pod.
Killer whales are always talking to one another
using a variety of whistling sounds, screams, and
squeals. We do not understand what the different
sounds mean, so we do not know what they are
saying. But the whales obviously understand
each other. If one animal uses a particular call,
another may respond with exactly the same call.

▲ Killer whales are
very curious and like
to know what is going
on around them.

Each killer whale pod has its own special range of calls. This is known as a "dialect." The killer whale calf will speak exactly the same dialect as its mother and its other close relatives in the pod.

◄ Killer whales often call to one another when they are traveling.

Learning to Hunt

As it grows older, the killer whale calf relies on its mother's milk less and less. Gradually, it starts eating solid food and begins to hunt with its mother and other members of the pod.

Killer whales eat a wide variety of prey, including squid, octopus, fish, sea turtles, otters, penguins, seals and sea lions, manatees, dolphins, and whales as large as blue whales. They have even been known to feed on land animals, such as moose and caribou, which are caught while trying to swim across the mouths of rivers.

▼ This killer whale is catching a young elephant seal.

KILLER WHALE FOOD CHAIN

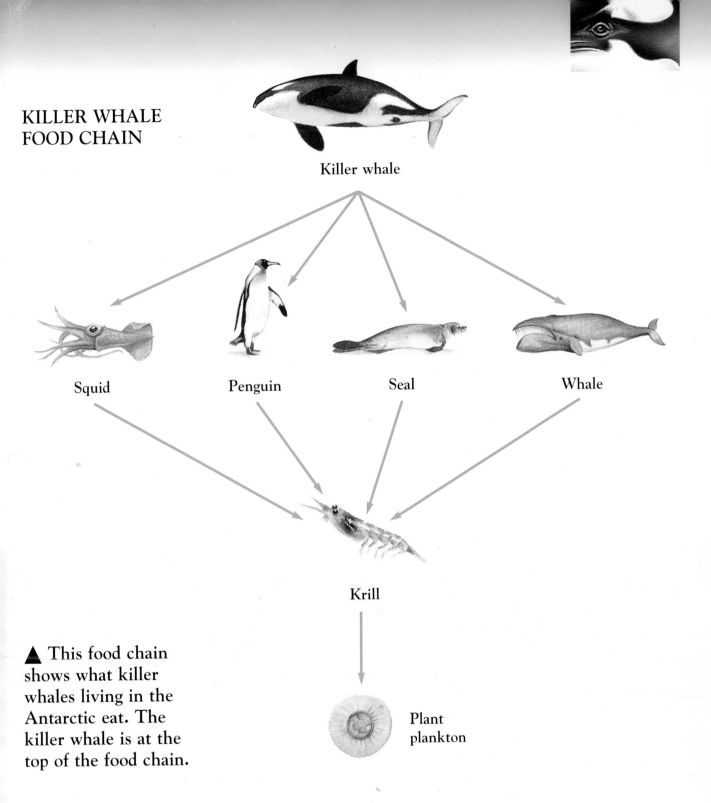

Killer whale

Squid

Penguin

Seal

Whale

Krill

Plant plankton

▲ This food chain shows what killer whales living in the Antarctic eat. The killer whale is at the top of the food chain.

Each killer whale pod tends to have its own favorite food. Fish is the most popular, but some pods eat mainly seals, dolphins, and other much larger animals.

▼ The family members of a pod normally hunt together, working as a team to find and catch their food.

WORKING WITH PEOPLE

Killer whales occasionally work with people when hunting. In the nineteenth century, a pod of killer whales at Twofold Bay, in New South Wales, Australia, used to alert the local whalers when right whales were passing by splashing the water with their tails. As a reward, the whalers threw the lips and tongues of the right whales they caught to the killer whales.

Hunting Together

It takes many years for a killer whale calf to learn how to hunt. Its family pod will use different hunting methods for different kinds of prey, and there is a great deal to learn. The calf learns by watching its older relatives at work and then trying to copy their technique. Sometimes, the adults will even give the youngster actual lessons.

Killer whales normally work together when they are hunting, rather like wolves hunting in a pack. In the Antarctic, they work together by tipping sleeping seals and penguins from ice floes into the waiting mouths of other members of the pod.

In other parts of the world, they even work in shifts to catch seals that hide in underwater caves. The whales take turns rising to the surface to breathe so that there are always some whales waiting when the seals finally have to leave their hiding places and go up for air.

▼ This killer whale is waiting for a penguin to jump into the water.

27

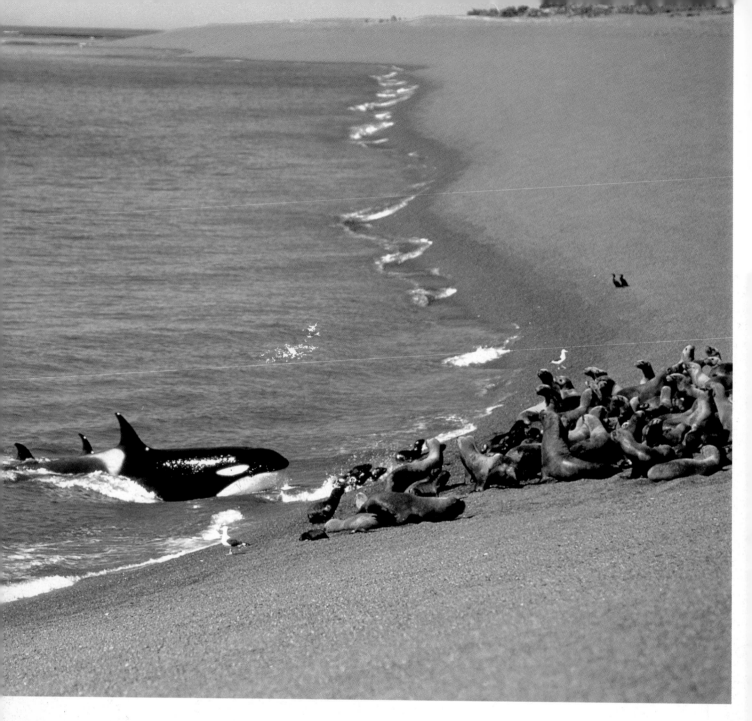

Killer Whales of Punta Norte

One of the most extraordinary hunting methods used by killer whales takes place along a remote beach in Argentina. At a place called Punta Norte, in Patagonia, several killer whale pods have learned how to catch sea lion pups and young elephant seals as they play in the shallows.

▲ An adult killer whale teaches two calves how to rush onto a beach in Argentina to catch young sea lions and elephant seals.

▼ When a killer whale rushes onto the beach, it is moving too fast for the sea lion pups to escape.

The whales cruise up and down in the water off the steep gravel beach, looking for suitable sea lions or elephant seals at the water's edge. When they have chosen their victim, one of the killer whales rushes toward the beach.

The whale moves so fast that it surges right out of the water. Most whales and dolphins are in serious trouble when they "strand" like this, but the killer whales of Punta Norte grab their prey and then wriggle back into the sea.

▼ Another successful hunt—this killer whale has captured a young sea lion pup.

Sound waves from
killer whale

Fish

Echoes
from fish

Killer whale

▲ Echolocation is very
useful at night and in
deep or muddy water,
where there is very
little light.

Finding Food

Killer whales can find their way around
underwater—and hunt their prey—without using
their eyes. They use a remarkable system called
"echolocation." The whales make special clicking
sounds and then listen for the echoes that bounce
back. These echoes may come from the seabed,
other killer whales, prey animals such as fish or
squid, the underside of a boat, or from any other
object in the water. By listening very carefully to
the echoes, and noting where they come from, the
whales build up a "sound picture" of their
underwater world.

Killer Whales and Humans

Killer whales have a fearsome reputation. Many people believe they kill everything in their path. It is true that they are capable of killing any animal in the sea, including great white sharks and even blue whales. But unlike many other large predators, wild killer whales are not dangerous to people.

▲ Many people believe that it is unnecessary and cruel to keep killer whales in captivity, in small concrete tanks, and to train them to perform tricks.

▼ Although killer whales are very powerful predators, they are normally very careful not to harm people.

There has been just one attack on a person in the wild. Many years ago, a surfer was attacked by a killer whale. But the whale had mistaken the surfer for a seal and spat him out. The surfer survived to tell the tale. No one knows why killer whales don't attack people.

Fully Grown

A killer whale has to be at least ten years old, and possibly as old as seventeen years, before it is able to breed. Killer whales probably choose their mates when two or more family pods gather together to form a superpod. These superpods can stay together for several minutes or hours at a time.

BREEDING

A female killer whale has a new calf roughly every five years—until she is about forty years old—although a few females keep on producing calves until they are well into their fifties. Typically, a female will have about six calves in her lifetime.

◀ Male killer whales have very tall, straight dorsal fins, whereas females have smaller, more curved fins.

▲ Killer whales of all ages seem to enjoy playing in the waves produced by a boat or ship.

When the different pods go their separate ways, the newly pregnant females are left to carry and look after the calves on their own. The males—the fathers—probably never meet their calves and do not play any part in raising them.

◀ Female killer whales can live to eighty or ninety years —as long as humans.

▼ A fully grown adult male breaching.

Old Age

Killer whales generally live a long time. As with humans, females tend to live longer than males. The longest a male can live is believed to be fifty to sixty years, whereas a female can probably live eighty to ninety years or even longer.

The older animals are very important in killer whale pods because they have great experience and can pass on their knowledge and skills to other members of the pod.

Threats

Unlike some other whales (see page 40), killer whales are not in danger of becoming extinct. They haven't been hunted in large numbers, although sometimes they are killed by fishermen or taken alive and kept in marine parks and zoos.

Yet killer whales face many different threats in the wild. Fishermen sometimes take too many fish, which threatens their food supplies. Dangerous pollutants from factories, farmland, and towns pour into the sea every day and threaten their health. In many parts of the world, killer whales are injured or killed by boat propellers and harmed by oil spills.

▼ If people take too many fish from the sea, there will not be enough food for whales, dolphins, and porpoises to eat.

KILLER WHALES IN CAPTIVITY

Killer whales have been kept in marine parks and zoos for nearly forty years. Some are born in captivity, but the vast majority are taken from their family pods in the wild. In their new homes they often have to live alone, in small concrete tanks, and are forced to eat dead fish. Many people believe that no more killer whales should be taken from the wild and that some of those in captivity should be released.

The film *Free Willy* made Keiko the killer whale famous. The film led to a campaign for his release back into the wild, to his home waters around Iceland.

▲ Keiko, the killer whale star of the film *Free Willy*

Threats to Other Whales

Some other whales are much more threatened than killer whales. Millions of large whales—such as the blue, fin, sei, humpback, and right—have been hunted and killed to produce oil, candles, soap, margarine, pet food, and many other products. Most large whales are now protected by law. Despite this, more than 1,000 minke whales are still being killed every year by Japan and Norway.

Whales and dolphins, including killer whales, sometimes strand themselves on beaches. No one knows why they do this. When whales strand they usually get stuck and die.

▲ Millions of large whales have been killed over the years, and now some species are so rare they could become extinct.

▶ In some countries, there are teams of trained volunteers who help stranded whales and dolphins back into the sea.

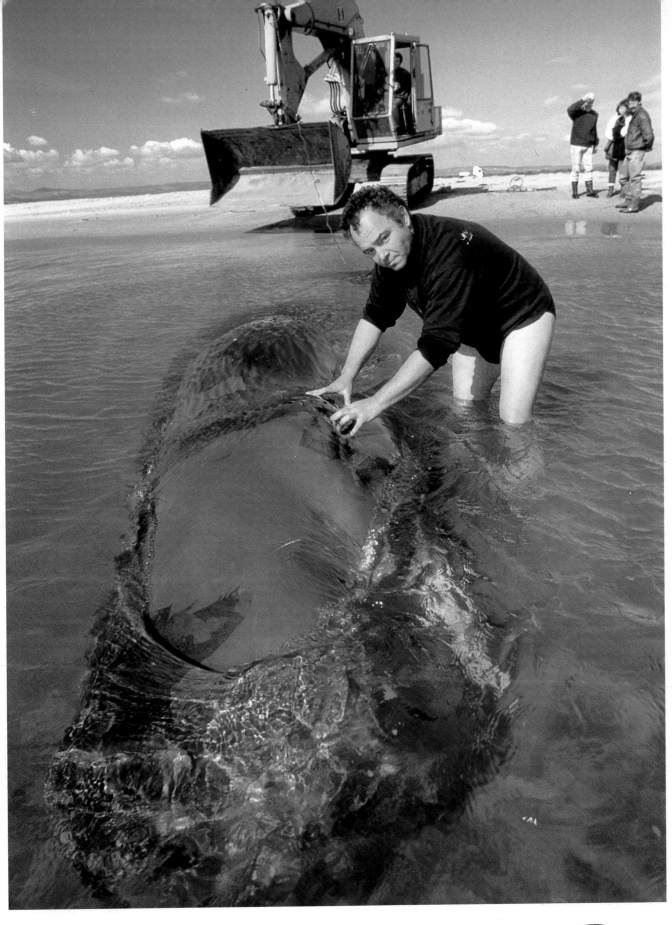

Protecting Killer Whales

Killer whales are quite widespread and, in some areas at least, still fairly common. But we do not know how well killer whales are coping with the many threats they face, so their future is still uncertain. The more we know about killer whales, the more we can help protect them.

One way to find out more about killer whales is to watch them in the wild on special boat trips.

▼ Watching killer whales in the wild is a very exciting experience.

▲ It is possible to watch wild killer whales in Canada, Argentina, Norway, Iceland, and many other places around the world.

You can help protect killer whales by adopting one through one of the many adoption projects available from wildlife conservation groups. This is a great way to learn about the lives of individual whales and to raise money for conservation at the same time.

You could also join a conservation group that works to protect killer whales and other whales and dolphins. There is a list of addresses on page 47.

Killer Whale Life Cycle

 1 When the killer whale calf is born, it measures from 6.5 ft. (2 m) to 8 ft. (2.5 m) in length— about a third the length of its mother.

2 After nearly two years of drinking its mother's milk, the young whale starts to take solid food and gradually learns how to hunt.

 3 In the first few years of its life, the calf learns how to catch food and how to communicate with other killer whales.

4 By the time it is ten years old, the whale is no longer a calf but a huge adult. Within a few years, the female will be ready to have a calf of its own.

5 After she has had five to six calves, the female killer whale stops breeding. The male will continue to breed for years to come.

6 Male killer whales live about fifty to sixty years. If they are lucky, females can live to eighty years or more.

Glossary

Blow The breath of a whale (also known as the "spout").

Blowhole The nose, or nostrils, of a whale.

Breaching Leaping high into the air and landing back in the water with a splash.

Dialect The special version of killer whale language unique to each pod.

Dorsal fin The fin on the back of a killer whale and most other whales, dolphins, and porpoises.

Marine Having to do with the sea. (A marine animal lives in the sea.)

Pod A family group of whales.

Polar The region around either the South Pole or the North Pole.

Predator An animal that hunts other animals for food.

Prey An animal that is hunted for food by other animals.

Strand To run aground.

Streamlined Shaped in such a way as to move easily through the water or the air.

Suckle To drink mother's milk.

Further Information

Web Sites

The Free Willy Keiko Foundation
http://www.keiko.org/home/
index.html

Keiko's official home page, with information, news and photos.

WhaleNet
http://whale.wheelock.edu/
An educational link focusing on whales and marine research.

Books to Read

Carwardine, Mark. *Whales, Dolphins and Porpoises*. Alexandria, VA: Time-Life Books, 1998.

Leon, Vicki. *A Pod of Killer Whales: The Mysterious and Beautiful Life of the Orcas*. New York: Silver Burdett Press, 1995.

Papastavrou, Vassili. *Whale (Eyewitness Guides)*. New York: Dorling Kindersley, 1993.

Parker, Steve. *Whales and Dolphins (Look Into Nature)*. San Francisco: Sierra Club Books, 1994.

Patent, Dorothy Hinshaw. *Killer Whales*. New York: Holiday House, 1993.

Index

All the numbers in **bold** refer to photographs or illustrations.